Old Mo

Written by Stacey W. Hsu
Illustrated by Adam Ritter

Children's Press®
A Division of Scholastic Inc.
New York • Toronto • London • Auckland • Sydney
Mexico City • New Delhi • Hong Kong
Danbury, Connecticut

For Nemo
–S.H.

For my mom, for always letting
me use her art supplies
–A.R.

Reading Consultant

Eileen Robinson
Reading Specialist

Library of Congress Cataloging-in-Publication Data

Hsu, Stacey W., 1973-
  Old Mo / written by Stacey W. Hsu ; illustrated by Adam Ritter.
     p. cm. — (A rookie reader)
  Summary: A boy describes the cat he loves.
  ISBN 0-516-24981-9 (lib. bdg.)   0-516-24762-X (pbk.)
  [1. Cats—Fiction. 2. Stories in rhyme.] I. Ritter, Adam, 1981- ill. II. Title. III. Series.
  PZ8.3.H84623Old 2006
  [E]—dc22

                                                                2005016145

CHILDREN'S PRESS, and A ROOKIE READER®, and associated logos are trademarks and/or
registered trademarks of Scholastic Library Publishing. SCHOLASTIC and associated logos are
trademarks and/or registered trademarks of Scholastic Inc.
1 2 3 4 5 6 7 8 9 10 R 15 14 13 12 11 10 09 08 07 06

I have a cat.

3

His name is Mo.

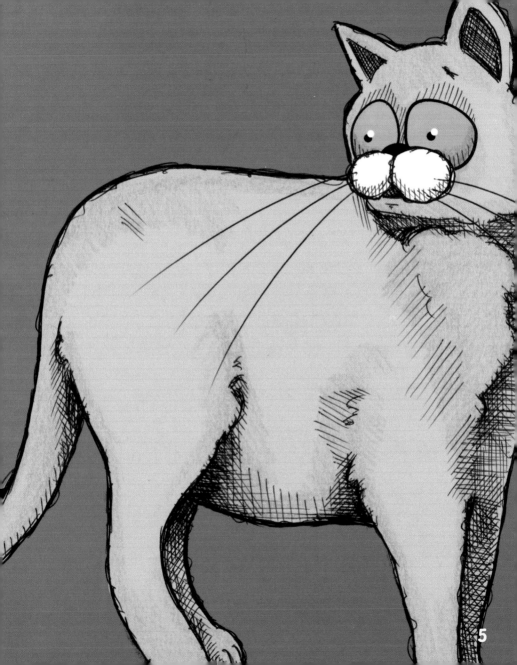

His nose is cold.

His green eyes glow!

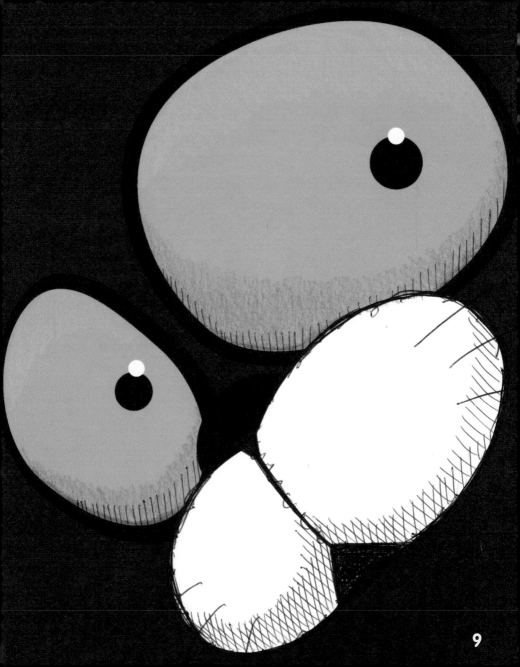

He flops on beds.

He flops on chairs.

He flops on me.

He flops on stairs.

He purrs really loudly.

He loves to sing.

He chases birds and other things.

He sleeps all day.

He prowls all night.

He loves to play.

He never bites.

I love old Mo.
He loves me, too.

This is how he tells me.
Mew!

Word List (46 Words)

(Words in **bold** are story words that rhyme.)

a
all
and
beds
birds
bites
cat
chairs
chases
cold
day
eyes
flops
glow
green
have

he
his
how
I
is
loudly
love
loves
me
mew
Mo
name
never
night
nose
old

on
other
play
prowls
purrs
really
sing
sleeps
stairs
tells
things
this
to
too

About the Author

Stacey Hsu is a writer and illustrator originally from Ada, Michigan. She currently lives in Kansas City, Kansas, with her husband, Chen, two very floppy cats, and a somewhat less floppy hamster.

About the Illustrator

Adam Ritter makes his debut as an illustrator with *Old Mo*. A former short-term employee of Scholastic Inc., Adam left an indelible impression with the company during his time there. Adam headed such work-morale-boosting programs as Women's Nutrition Oatmeal Mornings and Tie Mondays.